Copyright © December 2024 Carlette Lane

All rights reserved. This document is geared towards providing exact and reliable information about the topic and issue covered. The publication is sold because the publisher is not required to render accounting, officially permitted, or qualified services. If advice is necessary, legal or professional, a practiced individual in the profession should be ordered.

No part of this publication may be reproduced, duplicated, distributed, or transmitted in any form or by any means, including photocopying, recording, or other electronic or mechanical methods, without the prior written permission of the publisher, except in the case of brief quotations embodied in critical reviews and certain other noncommercial uses permitted by copyright law. Recording this publication is strictly prohibited and any storage of this document is not allowed unless with written permission from the publisher. All rights reserved.

The information provided herein is stated to be truthful and consistent, in that any liability, in terms of inattention or otherwise, by any usage or abuse of any policies, processes, or directions contained within is the solitary and utter responsibility of the recipient reader. Under no circumstances will any legal responsibility or blame be held against the publisher for any reparation, damages, or monetary loss due to the information herein, either directly or indirectly. Respective authors own all copyrights not held by the publisher.

Printed by Kiyanni B., Write It Out Publishing, LLC. in the United States of America.

Write It Out Publishing LLC
Virginia Beach, Virginia
Writeitoutpublishing.com

ISBN: 979-8-9919982-4-6

Book Cover Illustrator: Chris Negron

Editor: Tamira Butler-Likely

First printing, (e-book or paperback) December 2024
Author Carlette Lane
Virginia Beach, VA
smotheredpainbook@gmail.com
roarwomensministry.org

Smothered Pain

Breaking Free from the Shackles of Sin to Embrace Healing and Restoration

VIRGINIA BEACH, VA

Smothered Pain

BREAKING FREE FROM THE SHACKLES OF SIN TO EMBRACE
HEALING AND RESTORATION

Carlette Lane

FOREWORD

There is a unique power in a testimony. It is the bridge between where we've been and where we're called to go. It gives meaning to struggle and turns pain into purpose. In *Smothered Pain*, Carlette Lane courageously opens the door to her journey, offering a raw and unfiltered look at the depths of heartache and the heights of triumph.

This book is more than a collection of stories—it is a testament to the unshakable truth that with faith and trust in God, you can overcome anything. Carlette's words carry the weight of experience and the light of redemption. Her transparency is a gift, inviting readers to confront their own pain, lean into their faith, and find strength to persevere.

What makes *Smothered Pain* so profound is its honesty. Carlette does not shy away from the messy, complicated realities of life. Instead, she uses her voice to illuminate the path of healing, a journey anchored in God's grace and sustained by trust in His promises. This book reminds us that even when life feels suffocating, God's love can break through and breathe life into our weary souls.

As you turn the pages of this book, you will encounter testimonies that resonate, challenge, and inspire. Let Carlette's story remind you that triumph is possible, no matter how deep the pain. Let her faith encourage your own, and may her courage spark the courage in you to trust God with your journey.

Carlette Lane has written a book that will change lives. *Smothered Pain* is a message of hope, healing, and the miraculous power of a God who never abandons us. It is an honor to introduce this work to you and to invite you into its transformative pages.

With deep respect,

Matthew R. Cabler, MAML

"Carlette, I'll fill you up so you can pour into others to strengthen them. You are His beloved daughter, and you were called and chosen from your mother's womb." Many maintain Mordecai's rebuke to Esther as a guiding principle that conveys power and favor! Some maintain that the phrase "for such a time as this" represents something exceptional, chosen, or royal. In such a case, being transparent and sharing your journey is honorable, and it will annihilate yokes, strongholds, and shackles, ultimately destroying generational curses and rendering triumph, peace, and deliverance! No one can be delivered from what's hidden! Your openness demolished the enemy's arsenal: the impact of trauma, secrecy, and shame!

"This is the Lord's doing; it is marvelous in our eyes..."-Psalm 118:23

Rev. Deborah Brown

Carlette's story is one of resilience, recovery, and restoration. Her lived experience is a testimony of dealing with the harsh realities of a trauma-filled childhood and doing the work to become focused on dreams and visions of a fulfilled life of womanhood. Smothered Pain will inspire you to do better in order to be your best with every breath!

Rev. Marian D. Clifton, Assistant Professor

This heart-touching inspirational book is a testament of our spiritual daughter, Carlette. She shares the reality of the painful horrors of both mental and physical abuse. Her journey toward victory will inspire you to embrace the power of forgiveness and perseverance.

Pastor Lionel & Lady Beverly Goodwyn

NO MORE SECRETS

Effective Immediately:
All Generational Curses Broken

I've always been different. I have always felt this way, but I never knew how different I was until I remembered certain memories. As a little girl, I attended church with this lady, who we used to call Granny, on Church Street in Norfolk. This church had the hardest pews, and when we had the foot washing service, I knew we would be in church for at least another hour or so, #SMILING.

I also attended church with Mrs. Carolyn, my neighbor on Cumberland Street, also known as Whitaker Lane, in Youngs Park. We went to the Way of Truth Church of God in Christ on Maltby Avenue. At the tender age of eleven years old, I received the Holy Spirit. I will never forget that day. Little did I know, but my life would change forever. Roller coaster after roller coaster, but I have finally settled, somewhat.

Now, I understand why my life has been so peculiar. "But ye are a chosen generation, a royal priesthood, a holy nation, a peculiar people; that ye should shew forth the praises of him who hath called you out of darkness into his marvelous light" (1 Peter 2:9).

I've realized why everything that has happened in my life had to take place. Rejection, abandonment, failure, embarrassment, alcoholism, drug dealing, adultery, being violated (molested and raped), an accident, defamation of character, divorce, promiscuity, and looking for love in all the wrong places. I went through everything I went through for my children and my grandchildren. I am a generational curse destroyer! I am who I am, #myTruth!

THERE ARE LEVELS TO HEALING

"Forgive your parents for not having the ability to love you the way you needed to be loved. Now, forgive yourself for looking for love in all the wrong places."—Unknown Author

"When my father and my mother forsake me, then the Lord will take care of me."

Psalms 27:10

My mother was hanging out tonight, and I was at the house hoping she came home before he did. I was sleeping on the bottom bunk bed with a knife, and I believe I had a hammer underneath my pillow just in case he came in my room trying to mess with me. It is getting late. I am tired, and my eyelids are getting heavy. Am I dreaming? Someone is kissing on my legs and thighs, now my butt. My hand went to the knife (or hammer) under my pillow, then I smelled him. He always smelled like sweat and the drugs he took; it came out of his pores.

I flipped over and sat up in the bed with fear and anger. There he was, high on drugs, with his eyes wide and so big. In his hand was his uncircumcised penis, and he was playing with himself. I screamed as loud as I could like my mother was home, but she was not.

"GET OUT OF MY ROOM! GET OUT OF MY ROOM! I am going to tell my mama if you don't get out of my room," I screamed.

I called my big sister Caprice, who lived in California, and told her the entire story. So she paged my mom 911 to come home. I sat on my bunk bed, waiting for my mother to come home and rescue me. I thought to myself, "Tonight he is getting put out, and he is never coming back once I tell my mama what he tried to do to her daughter." That is what I thought. I heard my mom coming up the stairs, so I called out for her. Her scared daughter called out for her.

"Why are you crying?" she screamed. She was always screaming.

I told her the entire story. I told my mother everything in hopes that it would just be me and her from now on. Oh, and my uncle Jimmy now and then. Well, it did not happen the way I pictured it in my little head. I will NEVER forget her response. She said, "Do not tell anyone what you told me. What goes on in this house stays in this house." However, I just knew when I woke up, he would be gone, and things would be better in my and my mommy's life.

The next morning when I woke up, he was still at the house. SMOTHERED PAIN, I had to forgive my mother because she was hurt and damaged herself. She must have thought that no one else would or could give her real love, so she settled as many of us have done before.

***

The last time I saw my father was at 811. That is the jail in Norfolk. I asked him when he was coming home to take care of me, and he said soon. He never came home. I found out in 2017 that my father passed away in April 2000, one year before my mother passed away. That is all I can remember about my father.

Everything happens for a reason, which means that my life happened for a reason. The good, the bad, and the ugly were necessary. The rejection and abandonment were needed to push me into the woman God destined me to be. All the hurt and brokenness were a part of my destiny. Look at what Jesus said to Simon Peter when Peter asked Jesus if he was going to wash his feet.

John 13:6–7 says, "Then He came to Simon Peter. And Peter said to Him, 'Lord, are You washing my feet?' Jesus answered and said to him, 'What I am doing you do not understand now, but you will after this.'" When I was going through the trials and tribulations, there was no way you could've told me that "SOME" of my storms were to build tenacity and boldness in me, even down to my mother loving a hurt and damaged man. Yes, that was a part of my destiny as well.

Now let us be CLEAR: My mother was an AWESOME PROVIDER for her three girls. Do not let the smooth taste fool you. She made sure we were clean, had clothes on our backs, and had shoes on our feet. She also kept a clean house and we never skipped a meal. Even if it was beans and franks, we ate. Growing up in Youngs Park was a part of my destiny. When I was grown with two children, I received my own park house and moved to Calvary Square, better known as Curry Park. If you are not from Norfolk, you would not understand.

All my life was a part of my story of #BecomingCarlette. My journey made me into the woman I am and the woman I am becoming. Always remember that every person you meet, even down to your baby daddy, has a role to play in your life. Every storm, rejection, pain, hurt, trial, and tribulation has a purpose.

WATCH OUT NOW!

BOLDNESS of a LION!

"MY PARENTS"

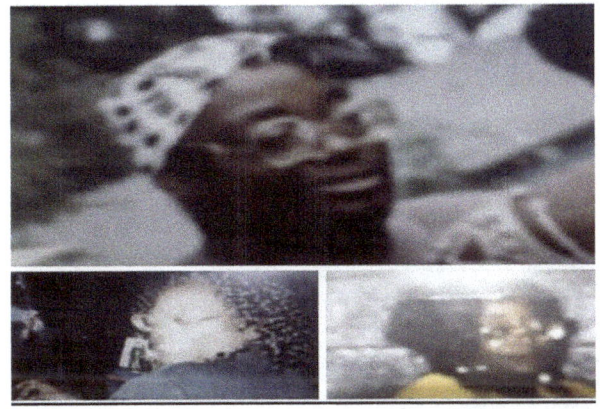

"MY PARENTS"

Elizabeth M. Lane aka NINA and
Carlton A. Lankford aka MOUTHPIECE

My Uncle Jimmy, my mother's only brother

He's the ONLY father figure I've ever had...

MY SISTER'S

Sharon, Caprice, Evelyn and ME

My children ♥ ♥ ♥

My grandchildren ♥ ♥ ♥

Amar & LaVette and Amani & Ava

ACKNOWLEDGMENTS

To my mother, **Elizabeth Mae Lane**,

I love you.

I miss you.

Most of all, I FORGIVE YOU.

To my father, **Carlton Alvin Lankford**,

I love you.

I miss you.

Daddy, I have been in search of a father all my life because you were not there. However, I have finally found the ultimate Father, God, and I FORGIVE YOU.

To my children, ***Amar*** and ***LaVette***,

I LOVE YOU TWO SO MUCH.

BOTH OF YOU ARE MY TRUE INSPIRATIONS.

Amar S. Lane, you are my strength.

LaVette C. Lane, you are my joy.

To my ANGELS, my two sisters,

Sharon Elizabeth Lane and **Evelyn Carla Lane**,

I love and miss you two so much.

#sistersheartsthatareinseparable

SMOTHERED PAIN

Chapter 1: Transformation: the Butterfly Effect	25
Chapter 2: Triggers, Trauma, And Trust	29
Chapter 3: And Another Round	33
Chapter 4: Wounds Need To Heal Properly	37
Chapter 5: The Process	39
Chapter 6: Girl, Keep Going	41
Chapter 7: I Love You, Daughter	43
Chapter 8: Tears	47

"The wicked flee when no one pursues, but the righteous are bold as a lion."

Proverbs 28:1

CHAPTER 1

TRANSFORMATION:
The Butterfly Effect

"Sometimes God will change your circle to change your life."—Unknown Author

Transformation: A thorough or dramatic change in form or appearance; extreme, radical change.

Spiritual transformation: Involves a fundamental change in a person's sacred or spiritual life.

The love I had for reggae music, dressing up, and going out to the club was crazy. I sold weed and stole clothes to assist with the $271 welfare check I received monthly to take care of me and my two children. My son's father was in prison and my daughter's father was only paying $50 every two weeks for child support.

My daughter was a newborn baby, around three or four months old, when they robbed me. I heard a knock on the screen door, so I answered it. I was familiar with the man at the door, but he wanted me to serve someone I was unfamiliar with (That is a no-no. You do not sell drugs to a person you do not know because you cannot trust everyone). I did it anyway for the love of money. I allowed him in, and as soon as I closed the door, he slapped me in my face with a pearl-handled gun. WOW!

The man I was familiar with had set me up to get robbed! I could not believe it! The burglar made me lay down on the floor, told me not to move, and he let his friend in the back door. Yes, there were two of them. Once he let his friend inside, they came over and asked me where the weed and money were.

I told them my children were in the house and not to hurt me. I gave them the bowl and all the money I had, but they were not satisfied. One of the robbers asked for the rest of the weed. He said, "Where are the ounces and pounds of weed at?" I lied and told them, "That is all I have!" The other one got upset and shot the gun in the house through the window while my daughter was on the bed sleeping. I was SCARED OUT OF MY MIND!

I screamed, "It is under the bed in the NIKE box!" At this point, my ears are ringing, and I am scared to death. They hog-tied me and said, "I would rape her, but she is on her period." They went out the back door. With tears in my eyes, I wiggled out of the hog-tie and went to look for my children. My daughter was still asleep, so I went to find my son. My son was upstairs in my mother's room in the corner by her bed, helpless with fear. I will never forget the look that was in my son's eyes.

Did I stop selling weed? NO, but I would not sell to unfamiliar people. CRAZY, right?

That should have been the last straw for me. However, it was not. After a while, I did stop selling weed. I woke up one day and realized that I had to do better with my life for myself and my children. So, I started attending a program through welfare called the Job Readiness Program. I started working and realized that the $271 I got once a month was nothing compared to the checks I was receiving every two weeks from getting up and going to work. That is when my transformation started.

My spiritual transformation started when I was a little girl. I was eleven years old when I first received the Holy Spirit at The Way of Truth Church of God in Christ in Norfolk, Virginia, where my pastor, at the time, was Pastor Wilbert McNair. My second transformation happened when I started attending church again in October 2000. I remember it like it was yesterday. It snowed that day, which made me smile. Tynema, my work friend, was the one who invited me to church.

She would not let up on me while we worked at Sentara Pace in Virginia Beach. So, one day, I told her YES, I would go to church with her. I attended the City of Refuge Church of God in Christ for seventeen years. This was the church where my gifts and callings were birthed. The pastor is Pastor Lionel V. Goodwyn, and he will always be my spiritual father. He taught me so much about myself, he and his lovely wife, First Lady Beverly Goodwyn.

My spiritual transformation is still occurring, and I will continue until the day God calls me home.

"And the LORD restored Job's losses when he prayed for his friends. Indeed, the LORD gave Job twice as much as he had before."

Job 42:1o

"Even in the most beautiful gardens, weeds and thorns grow and need to be pulled out so that the good plants can be healthy."—Unknown Author

CHAPTER 2

TRIGGERS, TRAUMA, AND TRUST

Triggers: Anything that reminds someone of previous trauma.

Trauma: A deeply distressing or disturbing experience.

Trust: Firm belief in the character, strength, or truth of someone/thing.

I have experienced so much trauma in my life it is crazy, but in all honesty, that trauma has made me the woman I am today. This woman I am today stands tall, and she is bold! Not to say she does not have her days of woe is me, but I love #BecomingCarlette.

My trauma was when my mother's boyfriend, of over twenty years, tried to harm me because he was harmed as a child. My trauma happened when the candy lady's son and a friend attempted to hurt me when I was a little girl because they were sick. My trauma was when my two children and I were homeless three times, and we had to live in separate houses. My trauma occurred when my daughter and I had to lay in a dark house because the power was off. After all, I did not have any money to pay Dominion Power.

My trauma was when I lost my house at 1539 Dungee Street. It was our first time living in a house, and the house was brand new. It had three bedrooms, two full bathrooms, and a half bathroom. It was 1,582 square feet on a 3,727 square foot lot in the Olde Huntersville area of Norfolk. I loved that house!

That house was proof that I could take care of my two children and pay all my bills by myself, even though I was a divorced woman. In the blink of an eye, three years later, my life had turned upside down. I told God YES and did my initial sermon, so I figured my life should be peaches and cream, NOT FALLING APART! My son's father was murdered. I mean, WHAT? WHY? I lost my job, I lost my house because I had no income, and now here we are, homeless again. I was TRIGGERED.

I began to drink like a fish and went back to the club. Yes, I was a minister in the club. Drinking Patrón and 1800 tequila like my mind was bad. The crazy thing is, when I would go to the club, my friends and people I knew would say, "You're the church lady! What are you doing in the club?" UNBELIEVABLE!

Even they knew I did not belong in the club drinking. They knew and saw that I had turned my life around and was living for the Lord. What did I learn from this situation? Just because God takes you through a storm does not mean you go back to the life He already freed you from. That will PREACH! Even the people who are not free YET will notice and wonder why you came back.

My trigger was that I was homeless again, so I went back to what was familiar to me; pain, alcohol, men, and the club. Instead, I should have prayed and waited on God. My trigger was that I lost another job, so I went back to what I was comfortable with when I should have just waited and prayed until God turned that situation around. My trigger was my son's father was murdered for no reason. More grief on top of grief, I did not even have time to heal from the death of my mother and two sisters. More triggers! Why, God? Do you not think I need a break?

Why should I trust a God who will not give me a break? HOW am I supposed to trust a God that will not give me a break? Trust a man, child, please. My stepfather, the man who was supposed to be my provider and protector, was sick himself. How could I trust a man when all I had ever seen were men hurting my mother, me, and, come to find out, my sisters too? God, how can you expect me to trust you when I cannot even see you and know if you are real? How can you expect me to trust you, God, when all you have allowed in my life is trauma and pain?

Slowly and surely, God softened my heart, feelings, and emotions. He changed my thinking (I am still working on my "stinking thinking," Elder Goss). I forgave all of them, but most of all, I forgave MYSELF! It is a daily task to keep my heart, feelings, emotions, and thinking under control, but I am doing it ONLY with God's help. I forgave all of them for myself. I had to free myself so that I would be able to work freely for God and help the next woman in a similar situation.

*"Have you not known? Have you not heard? The everlasting God, the L*ORD*, the Creator of the ends of the earth, neither faints nor is weary. His understanding is unsearchable. He gives power to the weak, and to those who have no might He increases strength. Even the youths shall faint and be weary, and the young men shall utterly fall, But those who wait on the L*ORD *shall renew their strength; They shall mount up with wings like eagles, they shall run and not be weary, they shall walk and not faint."*

Isaiah 40:28–31

"In order to love who you are, you cannot hate the experiences that shaped you."—Unknown Author

CHAPTER 3

AND ANOTHER ROUND

Ding, ding, ding, and another round! There are twelve rounds in a professional boxing match. Each round lasts, at the most, three minutes. Imagine fighting with a man all night long. You are tired, but you will not give up until you win!

This is how I felt. I cannot lose; I have to keep fighting! From dusk to dawn, imagine how many hours that was. Jacob fought with the manifestation of God all night long. It was only because of God's mercy that Jacob survived. I FEEL LIKE RUNNING!

The Bible says in Genesis 32:25, "When the man saw that he would not win the match, he touched Jacob's hip and wrenched it out of its socket. (It is the end of verse 26 for me!)... I will not let you go unless you bless me."

That is how we need to be with our dreams and prayers. God, I ain't about to let go until you bless me (Yes, that is Ebonics.). God, I will not give up on this prayer until you bring it to pass. God, I will not give up on this dream until you bring it to pass. Stop giving up so fast when things do not go your way (That is a Word.).

Maybe God has something else in store for you. There is a possibility He has seen something in the future that you did not see, so it had to happen the way it did. Maybe your time or season was up concerning that situation, so He took it from you. Could it be that we do not realize who God is in our lives?

Who is God to you?

To me, honey, He is not a higher being or all that other stuff people claim Him to be. He is my rock and my salvation! I do not pray to the universe, honey; I pray to my God. He has been my Jehovah Jireh, my provider! He has been my Jehovah Shalom, my peace in the midst of the storms! El Roi, the God who sees me and you! He's been Jehovah Shammah, The Lord is There! He's been there the entire time, in the good, bad, and the ugly. Who is God to you? Who do you say that God is?

***

Sometimes you have to praise your way out! God allows trouble because we were built to handle the trouble. Have you ever thought, "Why did God ask Satan the question, have you noticed my servant Job?" When God asks a question, it's rhetorical. God is all knowing; God in His sovereignty and wisdom initiated this test for Job. Could it be that God initiated your test? Yes, God took everything from Job. His wife even said curse God and die. His friends accused him of doing evil. Job knew in his heart that this was not the case, he was an innocent man. Job believed God no matter what.

"Then Jacob was left alone; and a Man wrestled with him until the breaking of day. Now when He saw that He did not prevail against him, He touched the socket of his hip; and the socket of Jacob's hip was out of joint as He wrestled with him. And He said, 'Let Me go, for the day breaks.' But he said, 'I will not let You go unless You bless me!' So He said to him, 'What is your name?' He said, 'Jacob.' And He said, 'Your name shall no longer be called Jacob, but Israel; for you have struggled with God and with men, and have prevailed.' Then Jacob asked, saying, 'Tell me Your name, I pray.' And He said, 'Why is it that you ask about My name?' And He blessed him there. So Jacob called the name of the place Peniel: 'For I have seen God face to face, and my life is preserved.'"

Genesis 32:24–30

CHAPTER 4

WOUNDS NEED TO HEAL PROPERLY

"Sometimes God will use your deepest pain to launch your greatest calling."—Unknown Author

"Fear not, for I am with you; Be not dismayed, for I am your God. I will strengthen you, Yes, I will help you, I will uphold you with My righteous right hand."—Isaiah 41:10

Wounds, rejection, abandonment, hurt, divorce, promiscuity, violation, molestation, jealousy, gossip, and lack in every area of my life. Could these issues and circumstances be a catalyst for drawing you closer to God? It is all a part of God's plan! Yes, even the pain was a part of God's plan for your life. Let's clean, cover, and uncover the wounds so that they will heal properly.

It's so much bigger than you and me.

"Carlette, I'll fill you up so you can pour into others to strengthen them." It is so much bigger than you and me. "Some of these storms you went through or will go through will have nothing to do with you. Some of these storms, trials, situations, and circumstances you will go through will be for you to help the next person." Again, it is bigger than you and me. Once we understand that and tell God YES, we will be okay #smiling.

These trials, tribulations, situations, and circumstances have built tenacity, character, dauntlessness, boldness, maturity, confidence, and the opportunity to grow spiritually. Paul said, "My grace is sufficient for you, for my strength is made perfect in weakness." I am sorry, but sometimes God will not heal the sickness or end the tribulations. The sickness and the tribulation will end up being a thorn in your flesh. You will just have to keep on walking with that lameness.

Yes, I am saying, "Sometimes God will not heal you from your affliction." God never removed the thorn in Paul's flesh. Paul prayed to God to remove it, but God never removed the thorn. Some of the highest blessings in our life come from God's power in the center of tribulations. God transforms, shapes, strengthens, and builds us through hardship.

CHAPTER 5

THE PROCESS

The process will not look like the promise, #smiling. It is a fixed fight! We always win! Before all of that, always remember this: The process will not look like the promise. The middle will try to take you out.

Quote:
"The hardest part of your journey is neither the start not the finish but the middle mile."–Unknown Author

The middle will make you want to give up. Being in the middle will make you want to throw in the towel. It will make you think that God left you and has forgotten all about you. The middle will make you THINK you are about to lose your mind. Do not keep those thoughts in your head.

You can remove those thoughts and replace them with something positive. For example, I am broke is replaced with: No, I am in between blessings. I do not have a job changes to: No, I am currently waiting on my new position. GOD WILL BLESS YOU! Always remember, it will not be comfortable in the middle.

It is not supposed to be. It will help build you. The middle will build that boldness and tenacity in you that you will need to survive. #BecomingYOU is what God is trying to get you to understand; the person God called you to be. Listen, this will not be peaches and cream or easy, but it will be worth it. I once preached a sermon at the City of Refuge, "The Process Will Not Look Like The Promise." This sermon has been my reminder; let it be your reminder also.

"But this is the covenant that I will make with the house of Israel after those days, says the Lord. I will put My law in their minds, and write it on their hearts, and I will be their God, and they shall be My people."

Jeremiah 31:33

CHAPTER 6

GIRL, KEEP GOING

Life will happen. Things will happen in your life that will make you smile. Life is going to happen. Things will happen in your life that will knock the breath out of you and make you sad. Remember this: After you have cried, sat in darkness, and cried some more, get up and thank God for the strength that He gave you to get through it all. Thank God for the sunshine and tsunamis you will have to go through. Why?

Why do I have to go through pain, hurt, heartbreak, and tsunamis? The reason is to build the person that God is trying to get you to be. My advice is to stop pushing back and accept what God is trying to do in your life. Keep going, keep moving, do not stop, and do not look back. This is where we mess up, when we look back or go back to what is familiar to us. When God removes something or someone from your life, do not go back and give it life. Leave it alone.

I was married on July 26, 2003, and divorced on March 11, 2011. I remember trying to make my marriage work, knowing that he was not my husband. I remember trying several times, but it never worked. Why? Because he was not my husband.

Some people stay in a marriage for the children or other unknown reasons, knowing that this is not their spouse. I will even make it plain. People stay in relationships, friendships, and "situationships," knowing that person is not the one, but because they are familiar, we settle. WHOA! No more settling!

It is okay to wait. I have to type this again for myself. Carlette L. Lane, girl, it is okay to wait. Smile while you wait. Sis, keep going. Keep smiling.

Do you see me smiling? Keep working, keep reaching, keep climbing, keep singing, keep worshipping, keeping trying, keep teaching, keep reaching, keep studying, keep dancing, keep seeking, keep declaring, keep decreeing, keep acknowledging, keep desiring, keep loving the unlovable folks, keep believing, keep running, keep writing, keep reading, keep praying, keep seeking, keep knocking, keep building that business, and keep making it happen. Y'ALL , JUST KEEP GOING!

"So do not fear, for I am with you; do not be dismayed, for I am your God. I will strengthen you and help you; I will uphold you with my righteous right hand."

Isaiah 41:10

CHAPTER 7

I LOVE YOU, DAUGHTER

God loves you so much more than you can ever imagine. I just love how much He loves me and makes me smile even when I do not want to. It is amazing how you can live most of your life not knowing what real love is, how it feels to have real love, or how it looks to have real love. Oh, and spend your life looking for love in all the wrong places. Honey child, sister girl was tired. Do you hear me? I was TIRED. I cannot say when I realized that God loved me and not a man in this world could ever love me as much as God loves me, but I finally realized it; I am glad I did.

Here is the thing: The ministry of Jesus was not about giving us 20/20 vision but about sight. Jesus was trying to teach us to partner with God's eyes. He was trying to wake us up to a whole new way of thinking, seeing, living, and perceiving. Maybe the purity of something is only limited by our ability to see it. Instead of looking for what is not here, we should stare long enough to see what is actually here. If we have anything to learn from the Pharisees, it is that we can stare God in the face and have absolutely no idea we are doing so.

Carlette, go on, girl, and confidently sit at the feet of Jesus. You are His beloved daughter, and you were called and chosen from your mother's womb.

No more looking for love in all the wrong places for me. It is all about letting real love find me. How can real love find you and me, you might ask? Real love can find us in the heart of God, being confident in ourselves, and being our best selves. Most important of all, in the heart of God. Healthy and Godly love is what I am giving and receiving from here on out.

Let us pray...

Father, direct us to understanding a new declaration that is found in you. May the assurance of our Father who lives inside of us fill our hearts with constant faith and trust. I am a woman on an assignment after you, Father, in full submission and complete dependency. I ask you to guide me as I work energetically and rest peacefully in your presence. God, we thank you that we don't smell like what we've been through. God, we thank you for your protection and covering us when danger was all around us. We will no longer smother the pain, rejection, abandonment, trauma, heartbreak, grief, hurt, or disappointment. We will give it all to you, God. You will heal us and help us to teach others how not to smother these issues. We thank you for your grace and mercy that are new every morning... Great is your faithfulness. Thank you for your powerful presence in our lives. We thank you that your heart is toward us, your eyes are over us, and your ears are open to our prayers. My job is to be that woman that you called and created me to be. Show me how to animate out my unique story and I will shadow you with fearlessness and the boldness of a lion #BecomingCarlette. Amen.

"Do not be afraid of sudden terror, nor of trouble from the wicked when it comes; For the Lord will be your confidence and will keep your foot from being caught."

Proverbs 3:25–26

CHAPTER 8

TEARS

To be honest, I trust God with every area of my life EXCEPT one. I don't, or should I say I didn't, trust God to send me my husband.

I've always dreamed of having a Priest, Provider, Protector, and Prayer Warrior as my husband. Did I really believe God would bless a wounded, damaged, broken, divorced woman like me? NO!

I see so many beautiful marriages, and I wonder, "Will that ever be me?" I know, I know, I'm on the outside looking in, but at least they have their significant other. I have to be honest and say my first husband was an excellent provider for me and my two children. We had other issues that led to our divorce.

Where is my prince charming, God? I used to think it was my daughter's father. I knew he would rescue me from the craziness in Youngs Park. I vaguely remember when my daughter's father moved to Maryland and I asked him if the kids and I could move there with him. We had our bags packed because he stated we could stay the weekend. I never told him about the abuse from the child molester,

I just needed a way out! Both my sisters had gone, so I was the only daughter left. I NEEDED TO BE RESCUED!

Friday came and left, Saturday came and left. He didn't answer my calls, but he was at the club with another woman. TRIGGER. Of course, I acted a pure fool and got thrown out of the club. That was it for me. There was no price charming, no one was going to rescue me, so I realized I had to do it myself for me and my two children.

Angry with God was an understatement. Shouldn't I be happy and safe too? Other things happened to me that made me build up this wall and not allow God in this area of my life. I stopped believing it would ever happen for me. I had to ask myself, if almost every man that has been in my life was dysfunctional, then something must be wrong with me. The only good man I knew that was a constant in my life was my uncle Jimmy. He was my father figure, he even walked me down the aisle when I got married. I LOVE MY UNCLE JIMMY!

I've prayed and cried, and I've even written letters in my Bible to God about the husband I needed Him to bless me with. Well, here I am, fifty-two years young and still single. Honestly, I don't know why, but I do believe that once I completely TRUST GOD in this area of my life, it will happen.

Carlette L. Lane, did you just type you don't believe God? Yes, I did. Guess what? We ALL have an area in our lives where we don't completely trust God. Think about it before you judge me. If you truly trusted God, would you be sleeping with that married man or any man that ain't your husband? Drinking like a fish to cover up what's really going on deep inside of you. Taking supplements to go to sleep. Gossiping about everybody all the time like you're the perfect lamb. Emotionally eating everything in sight and not getting to the root of the problem. Being envious, prideful, and just lazy. Laziness comes from carelessness about the commands and priorities of God, yet you continue to expect Him to bless you, but you're slothful.

We all lack trust in some areas of our lives. How can we fix trusting GOD more? With prayer and fasting, but we must shut all illegal doors physically and spiritually. Speak positively over your life and watch God turn your life around. Command the RIVERS of GOD to flow in your life. Command the RIVERS of GOD to flow out of your belly. MIGHTY GOD!!! LORD, LET THERE BE LIGHT IN EVERY PERSON'S LIFE WHO'S READING THIS BOOK... including the author.

It is better to trust in the Lord
Than to put confidence in man.

Psalm 118:8 NKJV

Listen to God
Be ready to do His will
What is God saying to you?

THE S.O.A.P. METHOD

Reading and Applying God's Word to Our Lives

SCRIPTURE

Choose a scripture or passage of scripture. Read the verse or verses in your bible. Write and highlight meaningful words, phrases, or scriptures that stand out or resonate with you.

OBSERVATION

Take a few moments and observe the passage of scripture you've read. What is the overall message of the passage? What truth can you learn? What do you feel God is showing you through His Word? Did you learn anything new?

APPLICATION

Reflect on how you can apply these scriptures to your daily life. How can you implement what you've read? What habits, attitudes, or changes do you need to make? What lessons can you take away from the reading?

PRAYER

Say a prayer in reference to the passage. In prayer, thank God and ask Him for wisdom and revelation to help you apply these truths to your life. What do you want to tell God as a result of what you've read?

Eric Ryan and Adam Lowry are the founders of the SOAP Method.

1 Samuel 3

9. Therefore Eli said to Samuel, "Go, lie, down; and it shall be, if He calls you, that you must say, 'Speak, Lord, for your servant hears.'" "So Samuel went and lay down in his place.

10. Now the Lord came and stood and called as at other times, "Samuel! Samuel!"

And Samuel answered, "Speak, for Your servant hears."

Sunday:
_____
_____
_____
_____

Monday:
_____
_____
_____
_____

Tuesday:
_____
_____

Wednesday:

Thursday:

Friday:

Saturday:

www.ingramcontent.com/pod-product-compliance
Lightning Source LLC
Chambersburg PA
CBHW071231160426
43196CB00012B/2482